SEV
TO MIRACLES

MW01142251

By

Phillip Rich

Ekklisia Prophetic Apostolic Ministries, Inc.

Published by Ekklisia Ministries
Copyright 2009 A. D.

Take note that the name satan is not capitalized. We choose not to acknowledge him, even to the point of violating grammatical rules

Table of Contents

SEVEN KEYS TO MIRACLES

2 Corinthians 12:1; "It is not expedient for me doubtless to glory. I will come to visions and revelations of the Lord."

Paul already had many visitations and revelations of the Lord, yet he was setting his faith for more visitations, more visions, and more revelations. He was speaking it out of his mouth. *"I will come to it. This is going to happen in my life."*

Sometime ago I began seeking the Lord concerning miracles and helping people enter into a greater miracle flow so they would be able to get miracles on their own (between them and God), along with receiving them in meetings and crusades. I want people to be able to receive at home, on the road while driving down the highway, at the grocery store. Wherever they need a miracle they should be able to receive one.

~Seven Keys To Miracles~

While I was sitting at the desk in a motel room seeking the Lord, I sensed Him come through the door. He came over, sat on the bed, and told me He was going to give me the secrets to help His people receive miracles. He outlined seven things, with the scriptures, that will help people enter into the miraculous power of God. He instructed me to share those seven keys to miracles with His children.

<u>DECLARE HIS WONDROUS WORKS</u>

The first thing we must do is declare His wondrous works. The Lord said, "*My people have to vocally speak out the wondrous works that I have done.*" We must speak out what God has already done in the past for us and for others.

Psalms 107:22-24; "And let them sacrifice the sacrifices of thanksgiving, and <u>declare</u> <u>his</u> <u>works</u> with rejoicing. They that go down to the sea in ships, that do business in great waters; These see the works of the LORD, and his wonders in the deep."

This scripture is saying that when you start declaring the works of God it is time to launch out. Start declaring the works of God and then step out into faith. Start declaring the miracles that God has done in the past and then start stepping out into deep waters.

Those who have declared His wondrous works and stepped out in faith will see the works of the Lord and His wonders in the deep. They will receive the miracles they need.

Can you remember something the Lord did for you in the past? Especially your salvation? Maybe a healing? There are wondrous works and we need to declare them. We have to think back to something that God did for us in the past. Has the Lord ever given you a financial miracle? Maybe He gave you a job in the past. I am not talking about what is happening to you right now.

I am talking about something good that God did for you yesterday. Something He did in days gone by. A financial miracle that came your way. A deliverance. A bill that got paid supernaturally. A loved one who got saved. A loved one who was touched. A loved one who was healed. Can you remember something that God has done? Start declaring it by speaking it out of your mouth.

Psalms 111:2; "The works of the LORD are great, sought out (studied) **of all them that have pleasure therein."**

This is about enjoying someone getting a miracle. Do you enjoy God saving, blessing or setting somebody free? If you enjoy it, seek after those things. Those who take pleasure in them will seek them. Is it wrong? No. Our God does those things. People who don't seek them will never see them things. Whatever you pursue you will possess. If you never pursue the works of God, you will never have the works of God. Obviously we are to pursue Him, but we are also supposed to pursue His works. It says in our scripture that it is sought out by him who takes pleasure in it. I take pleasure in God working. I take pleasure in God delivering, saving, setting free, healing, lifting up and meeting somebody's needs. I ask God to do those things and I seek after them.

Psalms 111:3-4; "His work is honourable and glorious: and his righteousness endureth for ever. He hath made his wonderful works to be remembered: the LORD is gracious and full of compassion."

The devil doesn't want the good things you have received to be remembered. If humans start remembering what good things God has already done, it will cause those things to manifest again. His works are not to be forgotten, yet many of us forget.

The devil comes along and brings to our remembrance the lack in our life. He will bring to our remembrance something that hasn't happened yet. He will bring to our remembrance a prophecy that hasn't been fulfilled, something that hasn't been healed, a need that has not been met yet. He thrusts that in front of us and makes us ungrateful. When we are ungrateful, we become negative, critical and judgmental. We literally step out of the supernatural into the natural realm and step away from miracles. We step away from wonders by forgetting the good things that God has done.

The Lord says He wants you to remember those things. After the great things God did in the Old Testament, the people would sometimes set up a memorial. If nothing else they would pile up a bunch of stones and give those stones a name. They did that so they could remember. It is kind of like tying a string around your finger. When they saw the pile of stones, they remembered that God had given them a miracle, a breakthrough there.

Psalms 111:5-6: "He hath given meat unto them that fear him: he will ever be mindful of his covenant. He hath shewed his people the power of his works, that he may give them the heritage of the heathen."

The reason He does signs, wonders and miracles in your life is to give you confidence to go out and win the lost. You know how awesome God is because you have experienced it. You now have boldness to run through a troop and leap over a wall. You have the boldness to stand in the face of a principality or a demonic spirit that is facing you and trying to get you to back down from what God has called you to do. If you have had some wonders, some works of God happen in your life, if you have some miracles under your belt then you will face that thing and say, *"In Jesus Name, I am going on through."*

Before David ever slew Goliath he rehearsed two past victories out loud in front of the king. *"There was a time when a lion overtook one of the lambs and through the power of the Lord I slew that lion and delivered the lamb. There was another time when a bear did the same thing. God's power came upon me and I overtook that bear. I slew that bear and delivered the lamb. The same God that gave me that power is going to come upon me again and I am going to slay this uncircumcised Philistine also."* [1] Do you see that by declaring what God had already done, it gave

---

[1] 1 Samuel 17:34-37

him boldness and a confidence to enter another miracle in his life?

It is time for us to say, *"He will do it again."* It is time for us to remember the good things. If you have ever had a visitation of the Lord, ever heard His voice, ever smelled His glorious presence, ever sensed Him all around you, ever had Him lift you up into heavenly places, ever experienced Him on another level then you need to start talking, thinking and speaking about it.

Ruth Ward Heflin had miracles, signs and wonders on a regular basis. They weren't happening in the ministry of others and people would come to her to ask how it happened that she had an ongoing ministry of signs, wonders and miracles. She told them it was because she talked about them all the time and whatever you talk about will manifest. She said that while she was talking about it, it would start happening again. When she started talking about gold dust, it would fall again; start talking about a miracle and someone in the congregation would start getting one; start talking about a healing and somebody would get healed.

The Lord told me to have the people start recording the works, the miracles He had given them. They must declare them, speak of them. If they would speak of them openly, He would perform them again on their behalf.

Psalms 143:5; "I remember the days of old; I meditate on all thy works; I muse on the work of thy hands."

There are two things David would do. He would meditate on the works of the Lord, the things he had seen God do. And he would muse on the works that he had seen God do.

Meditate means to mutter to yourself or in prayer to speak it to God again. "*Lord, I remember what you did last week when you did this and this. I thank you for it. Lord, I remember the time when I couldn't pay a bill and I sought your face. You brought the finances through supernaturally. I just want to thank you for it.*" That is meditating. While you are doing it, you stir it up in faith and get another miracle.

Muse means to ponder, to deeply consider that God has done miracles in your life. If He is the same yesterday, today and forever as Hebrews 13:8 declares He is, then He will do identically the same things. James 1:17 says there is not even a shadow of a change in Him. Malachi 3:6 says He is the Lord God and He changes not. This tells me that the miracles He gave me before, He will give to me again because He has not changed. Psalm 107:22-24 says if we will declare them, we will see them again. You will see the works and the wonders if you will declare what He has already done.

Can you remember a past miracle? A financial one, a physical miracle, a miracle in your family or with a loved one. Lift your hands and begin to thank Him for them and be specific.

SPIRITUAL AGREEMENT

Matthew 18:18-20; "Verily I say unto you, Whatsoever ye shall bind on earth shall be bound in heaven: and whatsoever ye shall loose on earth shall be loosed in heaven. Again I say unto you, That if two of you shall agree on earth as touching any thing that they shall ask, it shall be done for them of my Father which is in heaven. For where two or three are gathered together in my name, there am I in the midst of them."

The next thing God spoke to me about was coming into agreement corporately. This agreement is not what we have been taught. Agreement in the spirit is different than a mental assent or a mental acknowledgement.

Agreement comes from a Greek word, *sumphoneo*, from where we get our word symphony. It means to harmonize, to concur spirit to spirit. It happens when you get in the Holy Ghost and start hearing God about the same thing. You pray about something and two or three others stand up saying they heard the same thing. Guess what, *sumphoneo* is getting ready to happen. There is a harmonizing in the spirit.[2]

We have not understood this kind of agreement. We understand mental assenting. It is possible for someone to come, share a need with me and my spirit to connect with it. That can happen, but it usually doesn't very often. We do the hit and miss thing. It might happen and it might not. If it does happen it is based upon *"if any two of you shall agree on earth as touching anything they shall ask, it shall be done."* When shall it be done? When you come into a spirit agreement. Spirit agreement always gets the answer. That means your spirit connected with the Holy Spirit is harmonizing with someone else's spirit who is connected with the same Holy Spirit. You are all getting the same thing. It is making a wonderful sound in the spirit, a symphony unto God. You begin to release that and miracles happen.

---

[2] This is expanded on further in our booklet entitled <u>Symphony Glory</u>. Information on ordering this book may be found on the Tapes & Books page located at the end or by accessing our website, *www.ekklisiaministries.com.*

It works that way with the word of knowledge sometimes. You are sitting there saying in your own heart and spirit, "*God, I really need you to meet this need. I have been praying for this and I really trust you.*" All of a sudden a man or woman of God begins to pick up what is in your spirit and they begin to speak it out.

That is why a word of knowledge is so powerful. It brings you into spiritual agreement. That is why the prophetic is so powerful. It brings you into spiritual agreement with the person you are ministering to. That is also why I don't like for people to come and tell me everything about themselves because what they don't know is that they are hindering me. A prophet works off of revelation so it is better for me to hear it straight from God. At times I can still hear if the Holy Spirit is really moving on me when you share a need. If my spirit can hear it then I can make a connection with you.

This agreement is making a connection in the spirit. It is not just mentally saying, "*Okay, I agree,*" because you are still not harmonizing. There is still not a spirit harmony, not a spirit-to-spirit connection. It is the spirit-to-spirit connection that takes you into miracles. This is why it is important for all of us to hear God.

We should not just come and have the prophet hear God for us because that is not harmonizing. That is why we have a School of the Prophets[3] which teaches you to hear God for yourself. We don't just teach you how to hear God for others. We teach you how to hear God for yourself. If you can't hear God for yourself how are you going to have any confidence to hear God for others? I teach people to give themselves prophecies. If you can't even give yourself a half decent prophecy and do yourself any good, how are you going to do anybody else any good? If your prophecy is not good enough for you why should it be good enough for anybody else? I can't tell you how many times I will be sitting and hear the Lord speak to me, *"thus saith the Lord…"* I write it out because that was God talking to me.

God said, *"I am going to do this in your life. I am going to do that in your life. I am going to use you in this way, in that way. I am going to take you here and do this for you. I am going to raise you up and transform you. The power is going to flow through you. I am going to use you in a greater way."* I wrote it all down and dated it. Then a

---

[3] The School of the Prophets is a four-year correspondence course that will bring you into a fuller understanding of the prophetic in our lives. Information may be found at *www.ekklisiaministries.com*.

couple of months later two different prophets confirmed it almost word for word. As soon as they confirmed it, it was spiritual agreement and was a done deal. Confirmation is agreement in the spirit and will produce miracles.

God is trying to teach us something. We need to hear God for ourselves and then share what God is telling us until others say, "*I heard that same thing from God.*" Join hands at that point because there is a miracle about to happen. "*If any two of you shall agree on earth as touching anything it shall be done.*"[4] Anything sounds like miracles to me.

---

[4] Matthew 18:19

SPOKEN REVELATION PRODUCES MIRACLES

Next, the Lord spoke to me about the revelation of His Word that would produce miracles. We need to use and speak that revelation to ourselves, to our family, to others. It will produce miracles. The spoken revelation will produce a miracle.

2 Peter 1:3; "According as his divine power hath given unto us all things that pertain unto life [the natural] **and godliness** [the things of the spirit]**, through the knowledge** [or the revelation] **of him** [His Word] **that hath called us to glory and virtue:"**

The revelation of the Word releases the power of God to produce the miracles of God in your life. This revelation will get you all things that pertain to life and godliness. Revelation will get the stuff for us. Revelation will produce it. If we know that revelation is going to produce it, how do we get revelation?

2 Peter 1:19-21; "We have also a more sure word of prophecy; whereunto ye do well that ye take heed, as unto a light that shineth in a dark place, until the day dawn, and the day star arise in your hearts: Knowing this first, that no prophecy of the scripture is of any private interpretation. For the prophecy came not in old time by the will of man: but holy men of God spake as they were moved by the Holy Ghost."

Prophecy of scripture is the context here. Scripture is prophetic because it was spoken by prophets. It was God breathed, came out of God's mouth first. God prophesied it. Then the men and women of God prophesied it and wrote it down.

How do you get the revelation? Take heed to the Word of God. Study the Word. Meditate the Word. Read the Word. Go over the Word *"until the day dawn, and the day star arise in your hearts."* Stay in the Word until the day dawn. What day dawning? The miracle day. The day of manifestation. The day you have been waiting on. The day you have believed for. The day you have been reaching out for.

Take heed of the Word until the light shines. When revelation comes, light shines. Light and revelation are synonymous terms in the realm of the spirit. You do well if you take heed of the Word until revelation comes, because when revelation comes and you stay in it, your day will dawn. Your miracle day, your deliverance day will dawn. The thing you have been believing God to do is going to come.

The Lord said, *"Revelation of My Word will produce miracles."* He said to tell His people about the revelation of the Word. We have to take heed to the Word until the light shines, the day dawns and miracles are manifested. Let the light shine to dispel the darkness and the day will dawn. **Ps 107:20; "He sent his word, and healed them, and delivered them from their destructions."**

A revelation of God's Word will give you miracles, but you have to take heed as unto a light that shines. Take heed to the revelation until the day dawns. Keep looking at the revelation of the Word. Keep the revelation of the Word before your eyes. As long as you are looking at the light, your day will dawn. What light? The light of the revelation of the Word. I like to say it this way. You are one revelation away from a miracle, a healing, a financial breakthrough, seeing your family saved, a breakthrough in your ministry.

Each one of these things I am sharing with you can get you a miracle by itself. Can you imagine what would happen if you took all seven and used them? How quickly would your miracle happen and how powerful would it be?

ACQUIRE HIS PRESENCE

The fourth key to miracles is to do what it takes to get His presence in your midst wherever you are. Whenever you acquire His presence, you will acquire miracle power. In Luke 5:17, Jesus went into a house to teach and as He was teaching, the power of the Lord went forth to heal. That means His presence was bringing healing.

We have seen this happen for years. In the Benny Hinn meetings the presence of the Lord is there to heal. It is not Benny Hinn doing the healing. By the time those people get up on the platform, they are already healed. It happened while they were in their seats. The presence of the Lord healed them and Benny Hinn will be the first to tell you that. Get God's presence and you will get His miracles. All we have to do is stir up the presence of God and stir it up long enough.

This is the revelation that God put into Benny Hinn's heart, Kathryn Kuhlman's heart, and the hearts of others. Those who have this revelation and act on it know how to stir up the presence of God, how to get the presence of God to get healing and miracles. In the presence of God bondage cannot stay. Get a strong enough presence of God and demons just flee. Talk about deliverances. Shackles break, bondages break. I have heard demons coming out of people and nobody was laying hands on them. The presence of God was so thick that they came out. People would hit the floor and come up free.

God Inhabits Our Praise

Psalms 22:3; "But thou art holy, O thou that inhabitest the praises of Israel."

The Hebrew word for inhabitest is *Yaw-shab*. It means to sit down. In the Korean Bible this verse reads *"Let your praises build God a throne for Him to sit upon."* That is really what this verse is saying. You build Him a throne to sit upon.

We need to praise and worship, not till we are satisfied but until He is satisfied. You know when He is satisfied because He comes in. He shows up when He likes what He hears. It is very important that you hear this – it may only take 5 minutes or it may take five hours. If people press in, many times they can get His Presence fast when the throne is built adequately. Your praise and worship builds a throne for Him to sit upon.

The Throne and the Scepter

He will come and inspect the throne. You will feel Him move a little bit, but it is visitation at that point not habitation. Many mistake visitation for habitation. You are sensing Him there, but He is inspecting the throne to see if it is good enough. Did you build Him an adequate throne? Is He satisfied?

Jesus is the King of Kings, Lord of Lords. When a king sits upon the throne it has symbolic meaning. It means he is ruling and reigning over the whole domain. He is taking his place. When he sits down there is one more thing he does. Our King Jesus has a scepter.

Hebrews 1:8; "But unto the Son he saith, Thy throne, O God, is for ever and ever: a sceptre of righteousness is the sceptre of thy kingdom [of thy authority or rule]."

When a king sits down on his throne the first thing he does is take his scepter and hold it out. It means authority. He will start decreeing what is going to happen in that realm. He is going to decree what should and shouldn't be there. When Jesus sits down, He starts decreeing that there will be no sickness, no disease, no oppression, no depression, no demonic activity, no poverty allowed. He starts decreeing what there won't be. Then He starts decreeing what there will be. There will be full salvation, full deliverance, full healing, great blessing. When a king decrees it in a realm, it is done. The angels are His subjects who make it happen. Demonic heads are going to roll.

His Authority

So, when I get His presence I get His authority. When I get His presence I get Him taking authority over me and transferring authority to me. The Word says that as He is so are we in this world.[5] We are also kings and priests under King Jesus. We are going to rule and reign with Him. Not just someday, but now. Wherever Jesus comes in to rule and reign, we rule and reign with Him in that domain. The moment He has authority in a realm, we have authority in that realm.

---

[5] 1 John 4:17

When Jesus sits down, we sit down with Him. We are seated with Him in heavenly places. He will always decree when He sits down and we are to decree what He is already decreeing. It is all connected to His presence. Manifested presence is the glory of God. We begin to receive the presence of God because we praise, worship, communicate with Him and do what pleases Him.

Accommodate Him

If you want His presence, accommodate Him, give Him what He likes. If you will accommodate Him, He will accompany you. Give Him what He wants.

There are certain things He can't tolerate and won't show up for. If you have a bad attitude, He also won't show up. He won't show up for a bunch of negative words, for strife or a fighting spirit. He doesn't show up for fear, doubt and unbelief. If you want His presence, then discard everything that displeases Him from your life and give Him everything He likes.

Suppose the President wrote you a letter that he wanted to stay in your house or in your area. You would want to find out what kind of food he likes, make sure that you have everything he likes. We, as westerners, need to understand what the Jews understand about hospitability. You shouldn't just tell people they have to like what you have or lump it. That is not the way they do in the east. They will tell you that if there is anything you need and they don't have it, they will get it for you. Ask and they will go out of their way to give you what would make you comfortable, not just what you can get along with. As westerners we look at Jesus and tell Him that He is going to have to get along with what we like. That's western thinking and we wonder why we don't have the presence of God more in our lives. We wonder why we don't have more manifestations of God, more miracles. When you go to other countries that accommodate, you will notice that they have many more miracles we have.

Western thinking is "*all about me.*" We are a "*me first*" society. God doesn't like that kind of thinking. He won't accompany that kind of thinking. Remember, if you can get His presence, you can get His miracle working power in your behalf. I have been in churches where the power of God would come in, fill the place, and tumors and growths would disappear. Teeth would get filled. God would even grow teeth in for people. Organs that had been cut out would be put back. Missing body parts would be replaced. We didn't lay hands on anybody. That is what His presence does. His presence makes us whole.

God said to teach His people to do what it takes to get His presence and they would get miracles. That means anywhere, even driving down the highway. Put in a worship tape and sing to the Lord from your heart with it. If you don't have a worship tape, just sing from your heart. Make up love songs to Jesus. Your car will just fill up with Him. When you get His presence, you will get His miracle power. Do whatever it takes. Accommodate Him in whatever it takes. Do whatever He likes in whatever way He wants it and He will accompany you with His miracle presence.

FAITH AND BELIEVING

The next thing He told me was that faith and believing work together and never separately.

Mark 11:12-14; "And on the morrow, when they were come from Bethany, he was hungry: And seeing a fig tree afar off having leaves, he came, if haply he might find any thing thereon: and when he came to it, he found nothing but leaves; for the time of figs was not yet. And Jesus answered and said unto it, No man eat fruit of thee hereafter for ever. And his disciples heard it."

In Israel there are trees that have sap if they have leaves. If they have leaves and sap then they have fruit. There are fig trees that bear fruit year round. Other fig trees only bear fruit in certain seasons, but they don't have leaves either. Jesus knew that if they had leaves they should have fruit. The leaves were an outward show that they had something. If we claim to be a Christian, claim Jesus Christ as our Lord and Savior but we bear no fruit, we have already cursed ourselves and are ready to die from the roots up.

Jesus cursed the fig tree because it didn't bear fruit. If you don't bear fruit, you get cut off. We are supposed to be bearing fruit for Jesus.

Mark 11:20; "And in the morning, as they passed by, they saw the fig tree dried up from the roots."

He cursed the fig tree one day. The next day, twenty-four hours later, it was dried up from the roots. When He cursed the fig tree you could not tell that it had been cursed. Jesus didn't stand around asking, *"Father what has happened? I cursed it. I did what you had told me to do. When is this tree going to wither up?"* No, He cursed it and walked off. He knew it was a done deal. He knew the power of faith words and believing.

I want to tell you something about cancer. Cancer has its roots in the spirit realm and is not a pretty sight. If you were to see the spirit behind cancer you would see that demon is ugly. You can curse that spirit and you may not see a change. But in the spirit realm it is drying up and in time it will dry up in the natural as long as you don't stand around saying, *"I tried to believe,"* while you are looking at it. No, you already said something. Go on, it is done. Go about your business, Jesus did. Why? Because He had faith. He believed God.

Faith Produces Believing

Mark 11:21-22; *"And Peter calling to remembrance saith unto him, Master, behold, the fig tree which thou cursedst is withered away. And Jesus answering saith unto them, Have faith in God."*

Jesus is telling Peter how He did it. It started with faith in God. Faith has a noun tense. Faith is a person. You are having faith in Him. That is why you have substance. The substance is God. Believing has a verb tense. There are people who are trying to believe, but have no substance of faith. In other words, they don't have God in their heart or have faith in Him. If I don't have faith in Him, my believing is useless. Jesus said first to have faith in God. Later He talks about believing. It starts with faith in God. We need to read the Word, pray and have a relationship with God until we have faith in God.

Mark 11:23-24; "For verily I say unto you, That whosoever shall say unto this mountain, Be thou removed, and be thou cast into the sea; and shall not doubt in his heart, but shall

believe that those things which he saith shall come to pass; he shall have whatsoever he saith. Therefore I say unto you, What things soever ye desire, when ye pray, believe that ye receive them, and ye shall have them."

Believe. But believing starts with having faith in God. It starts with having the substance of faith, God in you. In Hebrews 11:1 we read *"Now faith is the substance."* The Greek word for faith is *pistis*, meaning to have confidence, trust, and reliance in somebody. Abraham believed God because He was the father of faith. He had God and that is why he could believe. You can't believe without faith because faith is your foundation for all believing.

There was a man who had been building up his faith in God. He heard God speak to him to take off his glasses and step on them. They were big thick bifocals. As soon as he did, he could see. Somebody standing next to him saw him go through the motions. So he took off his glasses, threw them down and stomped all over them. But he had to be led around because he couldn't see. Somebody had to take him home. One had believing without faith. The other had faith and believing. There is a difference.

Faith will lead you to an action, which is believing. People who believe with no faith will say things like, *"I was trying to believe."* They are really saying they had no faith because if they had faith they wouldn't be <u>trying</u> to believe. Faith empowers believing. It motivates believing. Faith pushes believing, is the substance of believing. It is the power to your believing. When faith is there you are not trying to believe, you are believing. It is that *"I know that I know that I know that I need to act on it."*

Get Faith

Where do you get it? Have faith in God. Abraham didn't have a Bible but he had God. He had faith because he had God. The Bible says he believed the things God said He was able to perform.[6]

I hold to the Word of God. I love it, read it, study it all the time. But if I never pray, never develop a relationship with God, then the Bible wouldn't do me any good. I know people who can quote more passages of scripture than you and I can. However, they have no relationship with Jesus Christ, so they have no faith. The Bible is

---

[6] Romans 4

supposed to connect you in a relationship with God. It is supposed to get you hooked up with God. When it does, you are going to have faith. How can you believe the Bible if you don't have confidence in the author?

Many years ago, my grandpa went into a bank and asked for a loan. They asked him how much money he needed and they gave him what he asked for. They knew him and what he said was good enough for them. I can believe the Bible because I know God. I have a relationship with Almighty God and I know He can't fail me. I know that He is more awesome than I could ever imagine. I know He cannot lie and not just because the Bible tells me, but because I met Him. I have confidence in what the book says, because I have confidence in Him. His Word is good to me, because He is good to me.

There is another level of faith that most people don't know anything about. I have heard people say that if you study and read the Bible, it is all you need to do to have faith. Wrong! That is only half of the equation. You need a relationship with Jesus Christ for your faith to be strong. Build a relationship with the Lord and His Word. Combine the two. That is why you have to have prayer and the Word. All Word dries you up. All prayer puffs you up. Put the two together and it will grow you up. Balance is the key to this thing. Balance the Word with a relationship with God. That means you have to read the Bible based upon a relationship with Him. This book should help you build a relationship. When you read it and study it, it helps you get closer to Him. It shows you what pleases Him. The bible helps you draw nigh unto Him. It bothers me when people take leather and paper and worship it. They don't know God. That book is about God. It is a Living Word. Do you know Him?

There are people who will get bent out of shape by what I just said. They don't understand that there is a living God. The Bible is to lead us to Him. Years ago I met a beautiful young lady and God said she was the one for me. *"Tell her she is the one and tell her exactly what I am telling you to tell her."* I went, told her and she said that it was exactly what God had told her. It would have been out of order for me to tell her all of that and for her to respond that God hadn't told her anything. At that point I would just have had to back off.

I would talk to her for an hour on the phone at my expense. A day or so later she would talk to me at her expense. I wrote one letter a week and she wrote one letter a week. At the time, I was in Bible College two hundred fifty miles away and had met her at a summer revival I had been holding. For about a year we would see each other once in awhile. We did a lot of talking on the phone and writing a lot of letters. I started developing a relationship with her over the phone. The letters were a very unique situation. I would get her letter, go into my bedroom, shut the door and lock it. As I read the letter I could hear her reading it to me. Because I had been talking to her on the phone I knew what she sounded like. I knew how she would say certain phrases. When I read the letter I picked up her voice inflections and her meaning. If you will build a close relationship with Jesus Christ, when you open His love letters you will hear His voice speaking to you the way He would say it. You will hear His voice inflections and understand the meaning. This is what the church-at-large is missing.

Jesus didn't say to have faith in His Word. He said to have faith in God. You can have faith in the Word because you have faith in the Author, the one who prophesied it, the one who said it. Jesus said to have faith in God and then believe.

This is what the Lord told me. If you want a miracle, start developing an intimacy with God. Start talking to Him, getting quiet, and letting Him talk to you. Then when you open His love letters, you will hear Him talking to you. You will hear the voice inflections. You will hear Him saying He is the lover of your soul.

Kathryn Kuhlman used to say, "*I believe in miracles because I believe in God*" and miracles would happen. She would walk out in front of the crowd and they could feel God walking out there with her.

Do you want an intimacy with God more than anything? Do you want Him to be your #1 love? Lift your hands and tell Him you want to fall in love with Him all over again.

FAITH TO FAITH

The Lord next spoke to me about adding faith to faith.

Ephesians 4:11-13; "And he gave some, apostles; and some, prophets; and some, evangelists; and some, pastors and teachers; For the perfecting of the saints, for the work of the ministry, for the edifying of the body of Christ: Till we all come in the unity of the faith, and of the knowledge of the Son of God, unto a perfect man, unto the measure of the stature of the fulness of Christ:"

Ephesians 4:16; "From whom the whole body fitly joined together and compacted [strengthened] **by that which every joint supplieth, according to the effectual working in the measure of every part, maketh increase of the body unto the edifying of itself in love."**

Notice, Paul is saying that each part, each joint is going to release strength to the other joints. That strength is a spiritual strength. It is releasing faith, power, glory, anointing. There are two things you have right now that the devil doesn't want you to know you have. If you know a little bit about them, then he tries to tell you that you don't have much of them. They are faith and anointing.

Faith and Anointing

Faith and anointing are not feelings. Anointing is an ability. Though the anointing can be felt, it is not a feeling. Anointing is the yoke destroying, burden removing power of God. 1 John 2:27 tells us that we have an anointing and we received it from the Lord. The anointing is the ability for you to do successfully what God has called you to do. We all have some, though some have more than others.

You have faith, though the devil wants to assure you that you don't have enough. Romans 12:3 says that each man has been given a measure of faith.

Romans 12:3; "For I say, through the grace given unto me, to every man that is among you, not to think of himself more highly than he

ought to think; but to think soberly, according as God hath dealt to every man the measure of faith."

We all know what a measuring cup is. We know what a teaspoon and a tablespoon are. Matthew 17 tells us that we have faith as a grain as mustard seed. Have you ever seen a grain of a mustard seed? It is very small, smaller than a BB pellet. If you take a sixteenth of a teaspoon and dip it into a jar of mustard seeds, how many would be on that measure of a teaspoon? A lot, possibly fifteen to twenty. Yet Jesus said, *"If you have faith as a mustard seed."* He said every man has been given a measure.

It only takes a mustard seed. The devil has been coming along telling us that it is going to take a dump truck of faith to get rid of a thimble full of problems. Jesus said it would only take a mustard seed to get rid of a mountain of problems. You have already been given a measure. You already have the faith. Most people don't exercise it. They don't continue to develop a relationship with God and as a result, they don't begin to act on their faith, which is believing.

One can chase a thousand, two can chase ten thousand. It keeps multiplying. If I add my faith to your faith, the two of us together have more faith than one of us does alone. The two faiths would produce more than the one faith would.

You have an anointing. I have an anointing. Anointing represents energy and power. Anointing also represents oil, which represents energy and power to do something. With my little bit of oil and your little bit of oil coupled together, we can do more. There is a lot more power and energy in the spirit than my anointing or your anointing by itself. Jesus was trying to teach us this.

Often we come together in a service and look to the minister who is preaching or teaching and want their faith to do it all. We want their anointing to do it all, so we drain, pull on them and put pressure on them. Then we wonder why a lot doesn't happen.

The very fact we do that drains some of the anointing, some of the faith out of the room. We hinder what God wants to do. We should be coming in with faith and adding faith to faith, agreeing in the spirit something is going to happen in the service. Somebody is going to get healed. Somebody is going to get blessed. Somebody is going to get delivered. A miracle is going to happen for somebody. If not for somebody in the service, then it will happen for a loved one we are connected to.

Join Together For Miracles

What would happen if when we came into a service we said, *"God, I am believing with my brothers and sisters that you are going to do something. God, you can use that minister or not use that minister, but I believe something is going to happen. I am not going to sit back, look at that preacher and say, 'We don't see what he has tonight.'"*

I prayed for a lady one time and heard a name. She said that it was her brother. I told her that I saw him on the operating table at that moment and he had died. But because we were praying in agreement at that moment in the spirit, he would live. She didn't know anything about what was happening to him. This took place on a Sunday morning and it took faith for me to tell her that. People were looking at me like I was off the wall.

Sunday night she came back to church and couldn't wait to testify. Her brother had called her and told her that he had almost died on the operating table. An organ had exploded in his body. Just before they put him under, the doctors told him they didn't think they could save him. They said he was about to die. All of a sudden the doctors knew what to do. They said it was like God was guiding their hands. The man lived, called his sister and told her it was a miracle. She told him she already knew about it and he asked how. She said that a prophet had told her about it. He was surprised because he hadn't even told her yet. Your family members can get a miracle because of your presence in a service. They don't have to be in the service, as long as you are there to represent them.

Remember the Philippian jailer in Acts 16? He told Paul he wanted to be saved. Paul answered that not only would he be saved, but his household with him. House or household means sphere of influence. Everybody you know on a first name basis, everyone you care about is a part of your house. They don't even have to be part of your bloodline. The Bible says that the believer sanctifies the unbeliever in a family, in a sphere of influence. Co-workers you care about are under the influence of the Holy Ghost. They are sanctified by you, set apart for God to deal with them.

When we start connecting in the spirit, God starts moving. It is like electrical circuitry. If everything is connected just right and there are no short-circuits, the power will flow.

God's power is always on. The problem is that we are not making a complete circuit. In a service, if nobody is short-circuiting by fear, doubt and unbelief, a critical or judgmental attitude or sitting back and wanting everyone else's faith to do it, if everybody is connected, then the power flows all the way around and things start happening. Miracles will start being released. In a house, if one little wire short-circuits the electrical system, things will not work. It is time for us to come into the house of God and be one in the Lord. Come into the house of God in agreement, adding faith to faith, adding anointing to anointing, hear and press into God. We have to be ready to see something happen, be ready to receive.

<u>VOWS</u>

God spoke that there is another key to receiving miracles when you just can't seem to get one. What grieves God's heart is that it is also a secret to the church. The church doesn't even recognize it. Satan and his kingdom have worked overtime to keep it a secret. He has twisted it and done everything in the world to keep this out of the hands of God's people.

This secret weapon to miracles is called *"vows."* If you can catch the full truth about vows, you can get a miracle when no one else can get one.

Vow a Vow

Hannah went to the temple every year. She fasted, prayed, and wept on her face before God. *"God, I want a child. Open my womb. Give me a miracle."* She did this year after year after year and could not get a miracle, until she made a vow.

1 Samuel 1:11; "And she vowed a vow, and said, O LORD of hosts, if thou wilt indeed look on the affliction of thine handmaid, and remember me, and not forget thine handmaid, but wilt give unto thine handmaid a man child, then I will give him unto the LORD all the days of his life, and there shall no razor come upon his head."

Notice that she was not vowing what she had. She was vowing what she didn't have. A vow is not about substance. It is about faith. It is not about my offering. It is about my knowing that God is my source for everything including my seed. It is going to God when we want to operate the principles of seedtime and harvest. It is going to God and saying, *"You said you would give seed to the sower. I want to be a sower. Would you give me some seed?"* instead of saying, *"I can't afford to give. I can't…. I can't…"* You are right. You can't. The man who says he can give and the man who says he cannot give are both correct. When God taught me this, I quit giving my money away and started giving His away. I had found out that all the money was His. Since then I have been able to do some tremendous things for the Gospel. I have been able to fund the Gospel and build churches in other countries. It is unbelievable what

I have been able to fund into the Gospel, not because I have had it, but because my Father has it.

My daughter and I were in a service one time where a prophet was challenging everyone to give. When a prophet is moving in the prophetic flow he will challenge you to give. My daughter was sitting right next to me when the prophet asked for a certain amount. My daughter looked at me and said she wanted to give so badly. She didn't have the money, but she knew that I did. Would I give her the money to give? What do you think I did about that? I didn't refuse her. It touched my heart that she was selfless, not selfish, and wanted to give to God. I reached quickly into my wallet, pulled out the exact amount of money and handed it to her. When I did, God spoke and asked why I didn't treat Him like that when it came time to give. Why didn't I want to give so bad that I would say, *"Heavenly Father, I don't have it to give in this offering right now, but you do. Would you give me some seed to give?"*

Hannah didn't give what she had, she gave what God had. She said, *"God if you will give me, then I will give."* That is a vow. *"If you will put it in my hand..."*

Now, don't go around promising God something and then don't do it. That is dangerous. Don't spend the money He puts into your hand to give. If you want to hurt yourself real fast, spend on yourself what He gives you to give.

It is important to understand the concept here. Hannah made a vow and said, *"Lord, if you will give me a child I will give the child to you."* She followed through with that. She not only gave her child to the Lord, but God also did something else for her.

1 Samuel 1:20-21; "Wherefore it came to pass, when the time was come about after Hannah had conceived, that she bare a son, and called his name Samuel, saying, Because I have asked him of the LORD. And the man Elkanah, and all his house, went up to offer unto the LORD the yearly sacrifice, and his vow."

She learned vows from her husband. She saw her husband make a vow and God give him the money. He would pay it and then he would get a miracle. I had wondered where she had learned vows until the Lord showed me this passage of scripture. The best way to learn vows is from someone else who does it. Just to hear about it, you don't catch the concept. You have to be around somebody who does it and see the results of it before it will really rub off on you.

1 Samuel 2:21; "And the LORD visited Hannah, so that she conceived, and bare three sons and two daughters. And the child Samuel grew before the LORD."

It is important to know that when you make a vow, you are going to break into a miracle. Her womb kept opening up and she kept conceiving when before she had not been able.

I am sharing this for your benefit. I know this stuff and am operating in it. God is already blessing me. I operate in vows on a regular basis. When we can't seem to get a miracle any other way, my wife and I use the secret weapon of vows. We use it over and over again. This will help you when you have been fasting, praying, doing everything else that you know to do. It is a secret weapon. Once you use it you will see the breakthrough come.

Benefits of Vows

Job 22:27-28; "Thou shalt make thy prayer unto him, and he shall hear thee, and thou shalt pay thy vows. Thou shalt also decree a thing, and it shall be established unto thee: and the light shall shine upon thy ways."

Decree anything you want, anything you are believing for, anything you need. Decree a miracle, a healing, a deliverance for you or a family member. Once you have made your vow, you have decreeing power for a miracle.

"It shall be established unto thee." Once you decree it He will establish it.

"The light shall shine upon thy ways." You are going to know what to do. You will know what the will of God is. You will know what the next step is.

This is all connected to a vow. If you are in confusion and don't know what the next step is, a vow can break you into the light upon your pathway.

It is not just making a vow, but paying it also.

Psalms 50:14-15; "Offer unto God thanksgiving; and pay thy vows unto the most High: And call upon me in the day of trouble: I will deliver thee, and thou shalt glorify me."

If you make a vow and pay it, when you come into a place of trouble where you need a miracle, He will deliver you. It is based upon the paid vow.

Psalms 66:13-14; "I will go into thy house with burnt offerings: I will pay thee my vows, Which my lips have uttered, and my mouth hath spoken, when I was in trouble."

"Was in trouble." In other words, I am no longer in trouble. Why, because of the vow. When David made the vow God brought him out of trouble. Vows can destroy the power of princes that have been attacking you. They can destroy stronghold spirits off of your loved ones and your family, your finances. Can you see what a powerful secret weapon this is?

Several years ago, my son started hanging out with some young people from school who had a rock band. Talented on more than one instrument, able to sing and write music he was wanted by this band. They kept working on him and getting with him. Stuff started rubbing off on him from hanging out with that bunch. Before long he was making plans to be in this rock group. He did not tell us, but told his sister. She came and told us. I knew where that would lead him. I could already see his spirit changing. My wife and I said, "*It is vow time.*" We were praying and doing everything else, but we knew we needed a secret weapon for this. We prayed about an amount that we needed to vow and pay. We made the vow, got the offering together and sent it to a ministry that believed in vows, deliverance and in the power of God. With the offering we told what we wanted that vow to accomplish, our son free from that spirit. We wanted him delivered from the demonic thing that was trying to get hold of him. We mailed it in the morning. The same day, without telling him what we had done, our son broke down and started weeping. He knew he was away from God. He didn't want to do that anymore. He didn't want to go that direction. He knew it was not right and never joined the rock group.

We have done this for every one of our children. When they hit a tough spot we activate the secret weapon. In our own lives when we hit a spot where we don't know what to do, we activate the secret weapon. When we have fasted, prayed and done everything we know to do and the breakthrough is not coming, we activate the secret weapon. We get a breakthrough every time. It wouldn't be right for me not to tell you what works in my life. God wanted me to share with you that there is a secret weapon for miracles. Use it as often as you need one.

CONCLUSION

These are seven keys to miracles the Lord shared with me and instructed me to share with you. Are you ready for a miracle? Are you ready for miracles to occur in your life on a regular basis?

Made in the USA
Charleston, SC
09 January 2014